SPIRITUAL MIND FOR LIFE

by

J. MAXIMILLIAN THURMOND

WWW.JMAXIMILLIAN.ORG

WWW.THEPREACHER.US

HTTP://THEPREACHER-JMAX.BLOGSPOT.COM

Therefore, brethren, stand fast, and hold the traditions which ye have been taught, whether by word, or our epistle. 2 Thes:2:15

Kingdom Novels

SPIRITUAL MIND FOR LIFE

Kingdom Novels is an imprint of

Whole Faith International Ministries, Inc.

For information address:

Kingdom Novels

P.O. Box 881064

Port St. Lucie, Florida 34988-1064

ISBN: 978-0-6151-4007-0

www.KingdomNovels.com

United States of America

Acknowledgments

I want to thank my Lord and Savior Jesus Christ for salvation and calling me to a higher place in Him as well as for my lovely wife, Gwandine; my son, Donnell; and my daughter, Morgan.

TM©

I will therefore that men pray everywhere, lifting up holy hands, without wrath and doubting. 1Tim:2:8

Dr. J. Maximillian Thurmond serves as the Senior Pastor of Whole Faith International Ministries, Inc. Located in Port Saint Lucie, Florida.

WH●LE FAI┼H MINISTRIES

VISIT US ONLINE TO VIEW OUR
CHURCH BROADCASTS AT:
WWW.WHOLEFAITH.ORG

My Testimony

I was in prison and the Lord Jesus filled me with His precious Holy Spirit during my incarceration. The Lord gave me a vision to minister to all nations as well as incarcerated people. Sometimes people feel unloved and forgotten. I'm a living testimony to inform you that God has not forgotten you! You are His peculiar treasure and the apple of His eye. There is nothing you have done that you cannot be forgiven of—no matter what anyone says because the Lord is a forgiving God. After you have received salvation and His forgiveness, you no longer need to feel condemned, for there is no condemnation in Christ Jesus. Rom:8:1.

Mankind was created in the image and likeness of God; made a little lower than the angels. Jesus loves you so much that He gave His life on Calvary. He was tortured, beaten, ridiculed, scoured, spat upon, including His flesh being ripped from his body with various cruel whips, and nailed upon a cross. Mk:10:34. Afterwards, Jesus rose from death on the third day and sprinkled His blood upon the Mercy Seat in the Holy of Holies to make atonement for the sins of mankind. God's word tells us that all have sinned and come short of the glory of God. Therefore, a sacrifice was necessary. Jesus became that sacrificial offering to wash away our sins. Heb:7:2. You can receive the Lord Jesus by first acknowledging that you were born in sin and shaped in iniquity (unrighteousness) and asking Him to forgive you and come into your heart. Commit yourself to the Lord Jesus by allowing Him to direct your path.

Afterwards, you need to be baptized into Jesus Christ by water immersion and be filled with the indwelling of the Holy Spirit, which is evidenced by speaking in other tongues (languages) as the Spirit of God gives the utterance. Jesus said that the Comforter (Holy Spirit) will teach you all things. Jn:14:26

Lastly, you need to live a holy life by putting off the works of the flesh such as lust, fornication, uncleanliness, unrighteousness, wickedness, covetousness, maliciousness, envy, jealously, strife, pride, murder, debate, deceit, whisperers, all lying, backbiting, swearing, all theft (including small items).

Begin telling others about what Christ did for you. Jesus promised us to dwell forever in the heavenly city called the New Jerusalem, which is to come. There will be no more death or sorrow. Rev:3:12

—Senior Pastor J. Maximillian Thurmond, D.Min.

CHAPTER ONE

Before you can develop your spiritual mind for life, you must first remove all evil prayers and thoughts you have against anyone. Reach deep inside and forgive everyone that you are holding a grudge against and let go of all bitterness. Who wants to eat the gall of bitterness? You can be the most anointed individual and will not lift off the ground to see Jesus in peace if you are holding an ought against anyone. There is no excuse! Jesus forgave all and requires us to do the same.

Do not curse individuals. Pray for their deliverance and salvation. God did not make us a vessel to curse. When you do this, you are assisting the enemy!

You will spend more time in eternity than in this present life. What are you setting yourself up for?

You need to clean your house (your earthly body). It is not kingdom worthy, nor kingdom minded to expend all your energy and effort trying to build a kingdom here in this present world. It would avail you to accept the Blood of

Jesus as your covering and not walk (live) according to the flesh (carnal nature).

Take on the attributes – the beatitudes of Jesus Christ. Pray to God, seek Him, study His word and be a doer of the word. Bring

every thought into captivity to the obedience of Christ. You can speak the word of God. You can include your name as you quote the scriptures to thwart off the enemy e.g., if Jane has the faith as a grain of a mustard seed, Jane can say unto this mountain be thou removed

or the Lord has prepared a place for _____ in the presence of mine enemies. You can quote this and use your name to fill in the blank. I am not saying to go and publish this to change the Bible. What I am saying is that you can do this to thwart the enemy and strengthen yourself.

Your main weapon against the devil is love. When you have the love of God for mankind, it becomes a powerful weapon against the enemy. When you pray for your enemies and mean it, and bless others rather than curse them, you become a threat to the devil.

Remember, we are in a spiritual battle. Christians must put up a resistance and be firm. It is similar to closing an executable file on the computer; except you are closing files in your mind. Another key factor is walking in humility. It takes self-control through the power of the Holy Spirit—not self-control by the will of your flesh. Flesh will fail you.

The Holy Spirit will not fail you. Walking in humility causes the flesh to be disgruntled. The flesh wants to get people "straight" and not take any stuff off anyone including spouses.

Sometimes in marriage, disagreements occur. However, if one spouse yields to the Holy Spirit, God will change hearts. I have witnessed a change in my wife and myself. The flesh wants to make its point, desires to be heard, and is quick to defend. This is not the attribute of our Lord and Savior, Jesus Christ. Jesus walked in humility. He did not try to defend Himself. Love is not proud, nor boastful, does not want its own way, and is not quick to point out someone else's faults. Love does not embarrass people.

If you consider your ways and walk in humility, God will raise you up. The Bible tells us that if we humble ourselves under the mighty hand of God, He will exalt us in due time. 1Pt:5:6.

I was the type of man that would not take anything off anyone. The Lord changed my heart and taught me to walk in humility.

Whatever we put in our spirit is what we will be. If you want your spirit man to be stronger, feed it. If you want your flesh to be stronger than your spirit man, feed it. How do you feed the spirit man? By fasting, praying and seeking the face of the Lord. Yes, fasting is still the 'in thing' with Jesus.

I know we live in a day and age where the church seldom fasts. However, fasting and praying in the Spirit is the key to strengthening your spirit man. Build up your spiritual immunity through word of God to resist the devil. Fasting tears down strongholds that the enemy has sown in your heart and spirit.

If you do not have a conversation nor seek the Lord on a daily basis, you will be out of character. Have you ever been around people, perhaps on the job and found yourself acting out of character? It is because you missed communing with Christ.

Your focal point should be Jesus at all times. Shut the door for carnality. Do not think nor speak things outside the word of God. Yes, ungodly thoughts will enter your heart. Do not dwell on them! Get rid of them immediately and apply the word of God. The Bible admonishes us that the devil resists those that are steadfast in the faith. It does not mean that the devil will not return later. Nevertheless, you can use that time to build yourself up in the faith by praying and fasting. Fasting helps bring your flesh under subjection. It gives you control over your flesh rather than allowing yourself to give into the lusts and desires of the flesh.

What are you putting in your spirit? Are you putting in godliness or carnality? You cannot be hot and cold at the same time. You have to be one or the other. Sometimes we miss the benefits of being Holy. There are great benefits to living Holy. Have you ever gotten the victory over your flesh during a time when you felt like telling someone off and chose not to? Nevertheless, rather than do evil, you did a kind gesture to the individual, e.g., saying something polite when your flesh wanted you to say or do something evil.

If you draw closer to God, He will draw closer to you. If you are not walking in obedience to God, you will not obey His word. Allow the Holy Spirit to direct your path rather than obeying the flesh. The flesh operates in envy, jealously, malice, greed, whispering, backbiting, lust, murder, hatred, strife, adultery, abominations, fornication and the like.

When you are obedient to God, you will not have to ask for things. Do not badger God about things repeatedly. God knows your heartfelt desires. If you are walking upright before Him, He will automatically give you the desires of your heart. The blessings are not the material things. The blessing is Jesus Christ and being in heavenly places with Him. In other words, being in a place with Him that should your life be required any moment, you have an assurance that you will spend eternity in the City of the New Jerusalem, which is to come.

CHAPTER TWO

When you think about things, you can actually make three-dimensional images appear. Our imagination can get us into trouble. Our imagination opens the door to demonic spirits.

We can allow demonic spirits to enter that allow us to tap into sensuality. You can have hidden sexual sins and no one would ever know. There was a time when pornography was obvious. An individual would be easily observed when entering those types of establishments. Nowadays, these sins can be hidden or camouflaged.

It starts to distort our natural desires for sex. People are being taught that it is natural to fondle oneself even in the schools. Our children are being taught this foolishness. This exalts itself above the knowledge of God. Some individuals cannot do anything without marijuana, sex toys, and other paraphernalia rather than being natural. It starts the individual to become gradually possessed.

Oral sex takes over the relationship. It starts to control your life. If you like to watch, when you get married, it will return to haunt you. It will excite your members and your sensuality. It is a trick and stronghold of the devil. It is addictive. It is your imagination.

Your imagination will take you to levels where you cannot cope with being around people that are gay, people that wear their pants pulled down, etc. The imagination will get you into a dilemma. We are not to change the individual – just minister the word of God. We are not to become personally involved with them.

Romans 1:21 tells us that *"Because that, when they knew God, they glorified Him not as God, neither were thankful, but became vain in their imaginations, and their foolish heart was darkened."*

This is the beginning of walking away from God. You can form mental pictures. If you can see it, you can become it! It starts to turn into a demonic form of idolatry. One should not take on sensual spirits when it comes to looking upon things and having fantasies, e.g., women having fantasies about being with a man in uniform or experiencing sensuality when it comes to seeing men's socks. I realize this sounds absurd, but stranger things have happened. You would be amazed at the things that tapping into sensuality can create. It is ungodly as well as an abomination.

You do not know what is going on in someone's imagination. In other words, how can I get away with this without anyone knowing? God knows. He knows the mind of man. We entertain evil spirits and welcome them by dwelling on this in our minds—we are supposed to cast this down!

Masturbation, oral sex, anal sex, homosexuality and lesbianism are all unclean. Just because something feels good, does not mean that it is good for you. The sensation that you feel is unnatural and is brought about by demonic spirits creating a false feeling that you think is you, and it is not you!

We are married to Jesus. He has set up His tabernacle on the inside of us to be Holy. He is our husbandman. We cannot walk in these secular, sensual, sexual desires and expect to be saved. The things in our imagination have risen against the things of God. God never intended for anyone to produce a sexual feeling by fondling himself or herself nor produce it mentally by unnatural ungodly means. It is demonic and idolatry. The Bible tells us to "flee idolatry!"

After a while, you will begin to dismiss seeking God and crying before Him. You must start dismissing the imagination and constantly pull down strongholds to serve the King of Glory—Jesus Christ. The Bible tells us as a man thinks in his heart, so is he. What you start to believe in your mind will begin to manifest itself outwardly. That is why you must profess the word of God over your life daily.

Secular (unsaved) people do not care about the word of God. People pray and confess Christ and do not desire to be saved. Their nature does not change. They have to desire and put forth a strong effort to change. The devil will continue to attack our minds until we depart this present world. We must cast down imaginations all the days of our lives.

Do not take advantage of helpless individuals, nor anyone else. People are children of God and are to be looked upon as such – not prey. We try to act as little gods by trying to shape and mold them into what we want them to be. That is God's job. We are here to give godly advice through His word. It is just our imagination. It is an attack of the enemy to steer us away from God. God is allowing things to rise up in us to turn it around in our lives so that we can live up to His standards.

We are going to have to cast down imaginations. The devil will try to make you believe that this is what you desire. The devil is a liar and the accuser of the brethren.

This will not overtake us like a flood – not if we cast down our imaginations. The Lord will raise up a standard against the flood of the enemy. Cast down all imaginations. It is a trick of the enemy. It is not real. It is just an illusion. You do not really want to do this!

Guard your heart, for out of it comes the issues of life. If you attend the movies, guard your heart from the erotic scenes. Albeit, I do not know how anyone professing Christ can watch certain movies. Some movies are designed to arouse and stimulate your sensual nature. There are some things that should not be portrayed on the screen. It does not matter whether you are an adult. You still need to guard your mind and allow the word of God to purify your heart. It's is just your imagination!

CHAPTER THREE

We are living in a day where there seems to be much turmoil and very few people that have the peace of God including saints. Saints characters are under attack. There is an actual character assassination going on inwardly.

Romans 15:38 references the God of Peace in which the Hebrew word is Shalom. Though your spirit is being attacked, you can have the peace of God. It is the peace of God that makes you whole. You have the entirety of God when you have the peace of God. In the time of trouble, you can have peace of mind and spirit.

Do not allow the enemy and the things of this world to shake you from your peace of God. Do not allow the fiery darts of the wicked to move you from your foundation in Jesus Christ. If you are going through something that shakes you from your peace, you are not focusing and meditating on God's promises.

An example is a piece of concrete being hammered then broken in pieces and chunks— something that was once whole. God has equipped us to quench the fiery darts of the wicked. There is a shield of protection called "faith" that protects us.

The Lord is my salvation and I will not be moved. You cannot be moved, shaken, and still be friendly. You can tell when some saints are going through. It shows in their countenance, gestures, and attitude. If you have the peace of God, you do not have to allow yourself to be shaken or moved. You do not have to be on the defense. Sometimes, you have to hold your peace. That makes you whole. The enemy's format is to break you down to nothing. You have to know when to hold your peace. Live peacefully with all people. Try to have harmonious relationships with all people.

Do not bring work situations home to your family. If you think about work while you are at home, pray and ask the Lord to free your mind and to help you dismiss those thoughts. Do not bring problems to your family unnecessarily. Sometimes, loved ones (not your immediate family) will call you from out of town and various places, and bear unpleasant things, e.g., Aunt Lula's cat drowned, etc.

There are people that cannot hold a conversation without complaining about how miserable their lives are. I have tried to help people like that and after a while; I realized they thrive on getting attention this way.

I do not care if it is "Aunt Lula" so to speak. You have to learn when to cut people off. My wife had an associate that would call her long distance to complain about her boyfriend and how terrible she thought he was. Finally, my wife explained to her that if the reason for her calling was to complain about her boyfriend, there was nothing further to discuss. She had the option of leaving this man. Of course, this woman was unsaved and did not want to receive sound advice. After that, the woman never called again. There are individuals that spend their entire lives creating misery for themselves.

A lot of this misery stems from the way they think. You do not need to entertain people like this because they will bring your spirit down and have you awake at night worrying, fasting, and praying while they are at resting and eating well. You can pray for them.

Sometimes, it is best to pray without them knowing it. The reason being, this can also be a way of them acquiring attention and utilize all your time by listening to their repetitive stories and requests for prayers. People have to want to change. I knew a sister in Christ that used to fast for people when saints would request her to do so until one day, one of my former pastors informed her to eat because he observed her requestor(s) eating at a restaurant when they were supposed to be fasting with her.

Parents do not need to share what they are going through with their children. Children have feelings too. They do not need to see their parents upset, frightened and worried. Parents need to be the right example of holiness to the Lord before their children. Even a small child watches their parent(s) and will sometimes mimic them. Let your child(ren) observe you praying to God and giving your problems to Him. Let them hear you make a confession of Jesus and profess the word of God. Let them witness you act in faith. Sometimes the most powerful witness you can give is to the members within your household that see you on a daily basis. They will know the real you—not just the *'church'* you!

CHAPTER FOUR

Let us go onto perfection. The word perfect means to be made whole. It signifies having reached its end; finished, complete, full-grown and mature. God made a covenant with Abraham. He told him to be perfect without blame. Christian conduct is not allowing your good to be evil spoken of. Rom:14:16.

You should not desire the life of fame and fortune. It will not lead you in the path of holiness. Jesus never preached fine houses and apparel. I am not saying that there is something wrong with having material things. I am speaking of desiring worldliness. You cannot mix oil and water.

Store up treasure in Heaven. The rich young ruler in Matt.19:16-22 did not want to sacrifice his possessions in order to inherit eternal life.

My wife and I gave up all. We forsook our house, land, family, cars and possessions to sojourn to a strange land. We traveled to Florida with a U-haul on a one-way trip where we had never been. The Lord let us know that He sent us to begin a ministry.

What you give up in this life—you store up in treasures. When you give up fleshly desires, lusts, etc., you store up treasure in Heaven. Whatever you sacrifice for Christ's sake in this life, He will reward you in this life along with treasures in Heaven. Be mature in Christ. Be whole in Christ, i.e., perfect.

CHAPTER FIVE

We have to understand that God is merciful. He gives us peace. We need to allow this to permeate within our spirit. We need the peace of God in our lives. I grew up with a lot of drama in my family including being a small boy attending school. There was always someone desiring to beat me up.

We do not need to create negativity in our thought processes. God has given us peace. There are people that God saved early in their lives. Some people God saved later in life. If you received salvation early in life, do not try to compare yourself with someone that received salvation later in life. Do not try to create problems unnecessarily. Be thankful that you did not have to suffer as someone that received salvation later in life possibly did. God does not want you to go through poverty, lack, etc. as someone may that does not know Jesus.

If you received salvation early in life, be thankful. Do not take on the mentality that you have to suffer the same things that someone else has. You do not have to sleep with "Johnny or Jane" in college and fail before you become successful simply because this may have happened to someone else.

You must understand whose child you are. You do not have to settle for being a stock person or a bagger the remainder of your life. You have to change the way you think. You have the favor of God in your life. You have God's favor operating in your life. Let the redeemed of the Lord say so whom He has redeemed from the hand of the enemy.

1Pt:1:18: Forasmuch as ye know that ye were not redeemed with corruptible things, as silver and gold, from your vain conversation received by tradition from your fathers;

Do you have to take this road? No! Do you have to live this lifestyle? No! It has nothing to do with the fact that you give healthy offerings or sow a special monetary seed. It has to do with the fact that Jesus redeemed you.

Acts:20:28: Take heed therefore unto yourselves, and to all the flock, over the which the Holy Ghost hath made you overseers, to feed the church of God, which he hath purchased with his own blood.

You do not have to struggle and start from the bottom like the world. You have the favor of God. He can elevate you if you have the faith to believe Him. Have faith in God. This is prosperity!

Prosperity does not come without a price. You have a right to be free from sin. You have been adopted into the royal family of God. You have been given dominion over the powers of darkness. You need to stay on the side of God, which is the victorious side.

We become wrapped-up in what we have been taught in various churches, that we always have to wait on God. You have already been set free! You have been redeemed from the hand of the enemy. You are Jesus' peculiar treasure. You have been bought with a price for His purchase.

Rv:5:9: And they sung a new song, saying, Thou art worthy to take the book, and to open the seals thereof: for thou wast slain, and hast redeemed us to God by thy blood out of every kindred, and tongue, and people, and nation;

God has people to be deacons, ushers, etc., which should be their humble side. In other words, you should love God so much that you will gladly clean the church or perform other layperson duties. You will not perform these duties the remainder of your life unless you choose to do so.

Sometimes church leaders become selfish and believe that God is sending people to clean their church. It is for the glory of God. That individual cleaning the church will not always perform that function. God will elevate them.

It is not our ministry. Pastors are not set up to be God. It is God's ministry and His work.

We do not have to be intimidated by our supervisors nor co-workers. God has not given us the spirit of fear. Are you intimidated by unsaved rich people? You have more going for you than they do in this life including the life to come. You possess more than they have. Know who you are in Christ. His mercy endures forever. And remember you have been redeemed from the hand of the enemy. You are free!

Rom:3:24: Being justified freely by his grace through the redemption that is in Christ Jesus.

CHAPTER SIX

Let us talk about envy. Some saints call it competition. The Bible calls it envy. There are saints in the church world that love to be envious. We need to hear from God. God is not going to tell you to copy everything in another person's life, e.g., every goal or accomplishment they have achieved.

Who wants to be challenged for everything they do? You will bring the other person down. It is a crying shame when saints are envious of children whose lives are going in a better direction than theirs. People will envy you in the name of Jesus!

Some adult saints will try to hinder the young ones from achieving their goals simply because their lives did not go in the direction they desired. Sometimes this is because they received salvation later in life. When many of the adult saints were younger, they were busy partying and you know the rest; they should have been setting and accomplishing goals for their lives. People will try to push you out of cleaning the church or ushering – simply from being envious.

Suppose the pastor makes a mistake and speaks highly of the usher or person performing their duties; I have observed people purposely stand and try to block the usher from performing his or her duties. I am a pastor and I work as a garbage man. This is unheard of. Pastors do not feel they should have this sort of trade. Instead, they want to teach prosperity while going to a devil's hell.

Envy is in the household. Brothers are getting jealous of their brother getting a new car. Sisters are getting jealous of their sister getting a new car in the family. It is a sin and a shame when a saint prospers and cannot stand in church and testify of God's goodness due to envy and jealously. It is also a shame when a saint cannot testify to their own parent(s) or siblings due to someone trying to compete with them due to envy.

Rom:13:13: Let us walk honestly, as in the day; not in rioting and drunkenness, not in chambering and wantonness, not in strife and envying.

1Cor:3:3: For ye are yet carnal: for whereas there is among you envying, and strife, and divisions, are ye not carnal, and walk as men?

The Lord blessed my wife and I to start a cleaning business and there was envy stemming from church members towards us. People were cursing us and hoping for our demise. People were giving demonic prophesies in the house of faith that we were going to lose our business, home, etc. We chose to give up everything to do the will of God. The Lord relocated us to Florida to get a new start and begin His ministry. We could have continued our cleaning business, which we did for a brief span until the Lord took us in a different direction to begin His work.

Envy is a yearning desire (a form of lust) to have what someone else has) to move like them, to walk like them, etc. I moved my wife and children to Florida and informed individuals in the state we formerly resided in that the Lord was blessing us to begin His ministry. Suddenly, it seemed as though everyone we shared our news with informed us that they were being led of the Lord to relocate to Florida and/or become involved in ministries and to start ministries.

Saints that heard prophesies that the Lord had given us concerning our future were trying to receive our prophesies for themselves. Some were even causing themselves to have dreams that the Lord had given them the exact prophesies that He gave my wife and I.

After this, my wife and I learned to keep whatever the Lord tells us to ourselves. It is a shame when you cannot share good news with others without them interrupting your rejoicing with their competitive stories. This should not be named by those of us professing Christ.

Be strong in the Lord. Know your God. Know how strong He is. Also, know the spiritual groupings associated with the spirit of envy. We need to know that the enemy is the devil and recognize his spiritual groupings and tactics.

Jms:3:16: For where envying and strife is, there is confusion and every evil work.

Job:5:2: For wrath killeth the foolish man, and envy slayeth the silly one.

Prov:30: A sound heart is the life of the flesh: but envy the rottenness of the bones.

The Bible admonishes us to rejoice with them that rejoice – not be envious!

CHAPTER SEVEN

Do not defile yourself. Stay free from the junk. Those things that proceed from the mouth defile the man.

Mt:15:19: For out of the heart proceed evil thoughts, murders, adulteries, fornications, thefts, false witness, blasphemies.

Things that proceed from the mouth defile the man. It is your heart. You are defiled if you always have a problem with adultery, fornication, covetousness, theft, bearing false witness, blasphemies, foul language, and the like.

Your heart is not right if you are having problems with the works of the flesh. Stay away from things that defile you. If you cannot stop watching pornography, you need to get clean and turn it over to God.

We make jokes about the following, e.g., when you make statements like, "That sandwich called me so I ate it." It really was calling you. It called to your fleshly lust.

Jesus paid the price for this. We want to entertain people that are defiled and place them in an auditorium. People that are defiled in the world go home at night and wonder how they can be delivered.

We are not planting enough seeds because we do not want to offend. However, we let the devil offend. When the individual is alone, they will think about that godly seed you sowed. The world thinks that if they label the music parental, this is acceptable. It is not okay for adults either.

It is like a virus when you watch, hear, and read blasphemies. It will overtake the good things that are in your spirit. You need to repent and be cleansed because it will try to bring back the old nature. It tries to give the fleshly (carnal) nature mouth-to-mouth resuscitation.

Once you take a stand – continue to stand! Do not give in to the devil being persistent. The enemy will try to tempt you with food-gluttony and other sins.

Do not allow any spirit to have you blaspheming, committing robbery, fornicating, committing adultery, etc. God gave you power to abstain from these things that defile your temple, which is the temple of the Holy Spirit.

You could be watching a good movie with hardly any curse words. However, the curse word(s) that they use are blasphemous. They take the Lord's name in vain!

You need to get rid of that! I do not care how good a movie is. I cannot associate with just anything because I will become engulfed in it. When I get involved in something, I am in it for the long haul.

You cannot entertain evil thoughts. If you open yourself up to any spirit, anything can happen, e.g., murder, adultery, fornication, etc. According to the word of God, you cannot say, pastor, I did not know this was happening. You entertained this thought and acted upon it. You did not just walk down the street and wind up in someone's bed committing sin.

There are evil spirits that inject thoughts to your mind to try you. They will ask whether you like the same sex. For out of the heart proceed evil thoughts. Whatever evil spirits can think of, they will try to defile your mind. Cast this foolishness down. Let this mind be in you, which was also in Christ Jesus.

Phil:2:5: Let this mind be in you, which was also in Christ Jesus.

Mt:15:18: But those things which proceed out of the mouth come forth from the heart; and they defile the man.

Mt:15:19: For out of the heart proceed evil thoughts, murders, adulteries, fornications, thefts, false witness, blasphemies:

Mk:7:20: And he said, That which cometh out of the man, that defileth the man.

21: For from within, out of the heart of men, proceed evil thoughts, adulteries, fornications, murders,

22: Thefts, covetousness, wickedness, deceit, lasciviousness, an evil eye, blasphemy, pride, foolishness:

23: All these evil things come from within, and defile the man.

You can cast down all of the evil imaginations. You can pull down every stronghold and every image! Let your mind be renewed. I choose to think on good things like souls being saved. Jesus made this very clear. Some saints say these things do not affect them. I find that difficult to believe because the Lord did not make me that way. I cannot be around nor dwell on certain things because they will adversely affect me by defiling my spirit.

CHAPTER EIGHT

Is there anything too hard for God? Why do thoughts (doubt) arise in your heart? We become troubled when we cannot see the blessings of God. We have a tendency to doubt and become troubled. You should always remain overtaken by the promises and not by what is going on in your surroundings.

Refusing to love others as Christ loved us causes doubt on top of doubt. We have to do what God says to do and no more. Only then can we walk in His divine order.

Why do we doubt God? Why do we doubt His word when we can dance and "amen" the preacher? We have to be careful when we start to doubt the word of God.

1Tm:2:8: I will therefore that men pray every where, lifting up holy hands, without wrath and doubting.

Every man has only two alternatives – to be on the side of the righteous or the unrighteous. Walking in the counsel of the ungodly is taking advice from someone who does not receive direction from the Lord. This causes doubt to creep in.

Saints should not mimic sinners, nor desire their ways. Saints must separate themselves from sinners. You must not gather with co-workers and poke fun at your supervisor along with the other co-workers.

The world is 'sometimey.' They will speak well of you as long as you are doing want they want. The moment you do something they do not like, they will speak evil of you.

Your delight is in the law of the Lord, and is His law do you meditate day and night. It delights me when I do what Jesus says. If you are a person that likes challenges – compete with yourself for your salvation. Seek to improve your walk with Christ by coming up higher in the Lord. Never compare yourself with others. When you do that, you can always find someone that is walking more carnal that yourself or vice versa.

Your goal should be to have your name remain in the Lamb's Book of Life. I make it my business to stay away from lukewarm saints. I do not closely associate with them. Some need to brush up on "God skills." Some need to know how to talk to people to be an effective witness.

Some saints cannot get this scripture right:
Ps:1:2: But his delight is in the law of the LORD; and in his law doth he meditate day and night.

Some are meditating on prosperity, their children's prosperity – rather than the word of God and the saving of souls. Most saints have the Jonah mentality. They are selfish and never desire to take on the good spirit of a person by speaking and acknowledging the good things about an individual. Instead, they choose to take on the bad attributes of the person and acknowledge the bad attributes of individuals.

We all have sinful desires that we like. Most saints will not admit this. We have been given the victory over this. You will not enter the gates of the Kingdom of God with sin. Secular people know individuals who act like Christians (saints).

They also know people who are Christians. They are not naïve because we are known by the fruit we bear.

It is an amazing thing to be written in the Lamb's Book of Life. I am thankful that God is alive! He is able to do abundantly above what we can ask or think.

As I previously explained, my wife and our children relocated to Florida with almost nothing. We could barely afford to make a one-way trip and had to leave most of our possessions (except our beds). We also had to leave our new beds. It was our original intent to start (or relocate) our cleaning business to Florida. I did not know whether we would be able to afford to live in the house we were renting in Florida during that time.

Jesus Christ made a way for us. Just the thought of arriving here to be able to rent a house caused me to have tears of joy because I reflected on a time when I used to be a Muslim and the fact that God delivered and saved me. I became appreciative of anything the Lord did for me. I come from a family that had Muslims. It was a trick of the enemy. I recall my mother believing that the Muslims were a good example for young men because they were well dressed and clean.

I received the Holy Spirit during the time of my incarceration. I was placed in what was called *The Hole* because a prison officer falsely accused me. There was a preacher there.

He had me to read scriptures pertaining to receiving the Holy Spirit and I began to speak with other tongues as the Spirit of God gave the utterance. Shortly after receiving the Holy Spirit, the preacher was removed from my location. I continued to speak in tongues for hours.

It is amazing to be in this position. I never had a man to train me in the word of God. It is God that humbled me. I had to pick up some nasty garbage in my employment position as a garbage man. I was informed during my hire that the position was a driver. They had to trust me to throw garbage before I became a driver. I am still working this job fulltime and serving as senior pastor to a new ministry God has called my wife and I to begin. My co-workers know that I am a pastor and the Lord has blessed me to witness with my life on this job.

Sometimes I am asked, "Preacher, what's the word of the day?" I give them the word of God.

I praise God for what He has done and is doing in my life. Praising God and living to please Him is the focal point of my life. Our lives are designed to praise God. We need to deny the flesh and give God the praise He deserves. Sometimes we have to take down and deny our flesh and trust God to work our situations out for His glory.

Sometimes we need to hold our peace. God will work things out. I go through a lot in my position as a garbage truck driver. Many times, I find myself having to be humble and let the glory of God shine forth.

We need to trust God and give Him the praise—even when you are on the job, He is with you. It is not always easy to give Him the praise, especially when you are going through situations where people are taking advantage of you and mistreating you.

This is the time to show forth the love of Christ to that individual. I explained to my wife once that we have to pray for those that despitefully use us. We have to pray the Lord's blessings upon their lives and not curse them. This is the humility that Jesus Christ displayed when He walked the Earth in a body of flesh.

Our flesh will tell us to get them told off and let them know that we do not have to take it. We cannot get them told off because that is operating in the flesh and will not get you into the God's Kingdom. Deny reacting in the flesh and show forth humility and the love of God.

—Praise God!

CHAPTER NINE

My son called me a hypocrite one day because I would treat him differently from others. I had to learn how to treat my son, wife, and daughter the way that I would speak to a pastor, an evangelist, etc.

My son's soul is just as important as someone being in the hospital bed, etc. A family member should have good things to say about one another. We have to give everyone the same treatment. Our character means a whole lot.

Be saintly. We like to pull people down and drag them through the mud. Sin has its way with us until we reflect who we are in the mind. You must have the word of God in your heart as the word of God explains – pull it from within you.

Many people viewed Jesus as being weak. He was not. I preached a message titled: Who Shall Deliver Me? If I would react in God rather than my flesh, they can look at me and see God.

Our minds need to be regenerated. The word of God is the opposite of sin. Regenerated means there was something else there. The world defines it differently, e.g., a remake of a song would have a hint of the old. Regenerated in Christ – there is no presence of the old man.

When God uses you – your soul will be blessed as well as others because you are doing His will. When we go against the flesh, we are recognizing Christ. Your mind (flesh) will tell you, "That's me—that's who I am," because it wants you to walk in carnality. No it is not who you are! God sees you as victorious. When your mind is regenerated, it is changed over from the natural to a spiritual mind.

Ti:3:5: Not by works of righteousness which we have done, but according to his mercy he saved us, by the washing of regeneration, and renewing of the Holy Ghost.

The word of God will change your mind as to how you view others. Sometimes, you have to speak the change of another person's mind. We have to do this through faith by walking, talking, and acting, as if it is God's will. If you have the heart for God and you have a particular desire, e.g., a job, God will make it His will for you.

This is why God brought you here – no more lessons – no more directions. Mankind is not concerned about your destiny. Nor is mankind concerned as to whether you walk or crawl. Sometimes, I feel like getting loud and praising God. They have this new thing now – do not make any noise and offend anyone. I get loud and praise God anyway.

When my family and I relocated, I did not know whether God was going to bless us. I had to learn to put off my fleshly mind. When the Holy Spirit steps in, God can change an individual in an instant.

We have to cease being hypocritical because we represent Christ. My son used to say, "If that is Christ, I don't want any part of it," because I was being a hypocrite. God spoke to me one day and told me to love my son. This bothered my flesh. I remained obedient.

One day I went to his home and he asked me, "How are you doing today dad?"

Now my son and I ride and work together. He refers to me as father because at one point, he wanted to address me by my first name.

CHAPTER TEN

Failure to yield to the Holy Spirit causes calamity. The Holy Ghost does not control your life. Neither is God going to change His word for you. You have to obey the word of God.

I had an accident while driving the garbage truck and the Lord spoke to me and said, "Failure to yield to the right of way." This experience ended up turning into a sermon.

You need to understand in doing His will, He will reveal more to you in this life. You have to fully yield to the Holy Spirit, fully give control, and fully submit. The Holy Spirit will drown out the flesh. Yielding to the Holy Spirit is simple. It is allowing the Holy Spirit the right of way. Before you can practice any of this, you have to turn your will over to the will of God. You must be filled with the Holy Spirit before you can do this.

You are in this life to be a servant of the most High God. If we walk through the doors that God has for us, it will elevate us. Be sober-minded. I am not speaking about being drunken. I am speaking of having the mind clear. If your focus is to be saved, you should not be focused on someone else's goals.

The Lord let me know that Sunday school is over—no more pats on the hand. God is calling for me to be that example and give of myself. I will have a Holy Ghost collision if I do not fulfill God's will.

Gird up the loins of your mind and cleanse your heart of all foolishness. Be sober – think on the things of God. You do not have to dwell on the future as far as desiring natural things. God will bring these things.

Pray for others. Others are supposed to pray for you. God wants us to work as a body. You have to believe just what His word says. We are more than conquerors. It is not feasible to inquire, "Why God?" Who can instruct God? Who knows the mind of God?

If you give the right of way to Jesus Christ and not give up, you will be successful in God. We were created to be a servant to Christ.

Do not allow anyone to use flattery as you are doing the will of God. Flattery comes before the kill! Do not get caught up in doing things to receive flattery. Give the glory to God. Do not listen to the flattery. Do not give ear nor heed to it. Remain focused on the word of God. Do not allow the enemy to cause you to lose focus. It only takes a second to get out of focus.

I Pt:13: Wherefore gird up the loins of your mind, be sober, and hope to the end for the grace that is to be brought unto you at the revelation of Jesus Christ;

I Pt:14: As obedient children, not fashioning yourselves according to the former lusts in your ignorance:

I Pt:15: But as he which hath called you is holy, so be ye holy in all manner of conversation;

I Pt:16: Because it is written, Be ye holy; for I am holy.

Sometimes, people will try to get you to take credit for what Jesus has done. You must immediately give Him glory and the credit because your flesh will try to step in and receive the flattery! There are many people professing salvation that are doing things for vain glory. You would be amazed at the masses of people that function in churches to receive a compliment or praise. There are people that refuse to do anything in the church unless they can get the chief seats and be in the forefront. Does this sound like you? The Bible warns us against the spirit of vain glory. Only what you do for Christ is what counts! The Scribes and Pharisees desired the uppermost seats in the synagogue. This is what Jesus spoke concerning the matter:

Gal:5:26: Let us not be desirous of vain glory, provoking one another, envying one another.

Mt:5:20: For I say unto you, That except your righteousness shall exceed the righteousness of the scribes and Pharisees, ye shall in no case enter into the kingdom of heaven.

CHAPTER ELEVEN

Fear—I Trust in the Lord! We need to stop fearing common elements. Fear brings on problems.

2Tm:1:7: For God hath not given us the spirit of fear; but of power, and of love, and of a sound mind.

Flesh tells us to fear; God tells us not to fear. Flesh tell us to worry about what we are going to eat and wear. We need to put this flesh down. One of my former pastors preached a message titled: A Bag of Excuses. Saints have excuses for everything. We are not supposed to walk in the flesh; we need to apply our spiritual antidote.

The fear of the Lord is wisdom. Do you trust Him? I trust the Lord in every aspect of my life. You really do not have a choice not to choose God. We blame others out of fear. People poke fun at others out of fear (their own insecurities).

The spirit of fear comes from the devil. Running from one thing or person to go to another thing or a person is due to fear. Examples are running from growth, getting older, dying, loss of limbs and receding hairlines, etc.

God makes a way of escape and He will raise a standard where we can run in and be safe.

Job:3:25: For the thing which I greatly feared is come upon me, and that which I was afraid of is come unto me.

We think that once we believe God for one form of fear, we have made it. Then another one comes along. The world always has a type of (runaway) solution, e.g., just run and go to another job. Fear will meet you there also.

Fear will cause you to throw off on other people by saying things that are offensive to them that you would not want said about you. Fear eats you up on the inside. Fear will have you in poverty – broke. Fear will stop you from obtaining a drivers license. I know of people to this day that have never obtained a drivers license due to fear. There are adults that do not have anything hindering them from learning to drive except one demon spirit – fear!

Where is your faith? Speak to that mountain and tell it to move.

Mt:17:20: And Jesus said unto them, Because of your unbelief: for verily I say unto you, If ye have faith as a grain of mustard seed, ye shall say unto this mountain, Remove hence to yonder place; and it shall remove; and nothing shall be impossible unto you.

I recall during my earlier days of learning to drive a commercial truck, I had a fear of learning to do this. I wanted to work recycle as a cop-out. Rather than do this, I decided to trust God. I decided not to run away from the circumstances. The Lord brought my truck driving together by simplifying my route.

2Kgs:6:16: And he answered, Fear not: for they that be with us are more than they that be with them.

When you lie down, you should not be afraid. The only way you can get rest is to have peace.

Prov:3:24: When thou liest down, thou shalt not be afraid: yea, thou shalt lie down, and thy sleep shall be sweet.

Fear makes you offended. Fear puts you on the defense. Fear will put on the defense when someone simply asks, "How are you doing?" Fear will make you think they are being nosey.

Ps:27:1: The LORD is my light and my salvation; whom shall I fear? the LORD is the strength of my life; of whom shall I be afraid?

Ps:27:3: Though an host should encamp against me, my heart shall not fear: though war should rise against me, in this will I be confident.

If we do not get it together with this flesh, it will overtake us. We need to do whatever it is we are going to do for God now! Stop being afraid of everything! Stop being fearful! God has everything under control.

Fear will distort the word of God to the point where you will not hear the word like you should. Jesus gives you peace that surpasses all understanding. You will not be offended when God gives you peace. Trust the Lord, He will be your confidence.

CHAPTER TWELVE

Make the Spiritual Connection. This woman had an issue. She could not perform as she wanted to. When you read the scriptures concerning the woman that had the issue of blood, remove the word blood and read it as 'this woman having an issue.' Then read the passage again.

If you have an issue, whether it is a job, a loved one, etc., stop trying to figure it out. If you are in the Spirit, you can receive whatever virtue Jesus sends to you. This woman had to be weak having this issue of blood for so long. This is how the enemy comes in. Nevertheless, if we focus on Jesus Christ, He will work it out.

God can bless and work it out and afterwards, another issue will arise. God can work that out too! God will resolve (solve) your issues. Do what God has given you to do.

Whatever your issue is, God can work it out whether it is mental, physical, etc.

This woman carried this issue for 12 years. You could carry it longer if your issue is not dealt with. It is not in spending your money; it is taking the problem to Jesus. She made a spiritual connection through her faith by touching the hem of Jesus' garment.

We all have issues and need to learn to touch the hem of Jesus' garment. Make the decision that this is what you want from God. Pursue it through Jesus. Jesus will bring it to pass.

Lk:8:43: And a woman having an issue of blood twelve years, which had spent all her living upon physicians, neither could be healed of any,

Lk:8:44: Came behind him, and touched the border of his garment: and immediately her issue of blood stanched.

Lk:8:45: And Jesus said, Who touched me? When all denied, Peter and they that were with him said, Master, the multitude throng thee and press thee, and sayest thou, Who touched me?

Lk:8:46: And Jesus said, Somebody hath touched me: for I perceive that virtue is gone out of me.

If you desire an increase in faith, it comes through the Holy Spirit and the heart of man. When you view God as being your everything, all you need to do is have full faith in who He is. You need to prepare yourself to bring your flesh under control to the Holy Spirit.

When you have been walking in your flesh, you have to bring your flesh under control. However, when you are walking in the Spirit, you do not have to prepare your flesh.

You have the right to "command ye me" according to your faith in God's word. You have to place your priorities in God's order. Pursue your requests through God.

Isa:45:11: Thus saith the LORD, the Holy One of Israel, and his Maker, Ask me of things to come concerning my sons, and concerning the work of my hands command ye me.

Your prophesy is on the way. Your blessings are on the way. When the Lord starts to bless and you receive words of prophesy, people will treat you differently. Sometimes it is family, church members and/or co-workers.

We all have gifts. When the gifts initially operate, it seems like a blessing. Afterwards, it seems to be a curse. This is why I do not allow people to give me nicknames. They make fun of you and mock you as Joseph was done. They said, "Behold, this dreamer cometh."

Gen:37:19: And they said one to another, Behold, this dreamer cometh.

When God gives you a prophesy, He does not tell you all the details. He does not tell you that your child will stop speaking to you or your spouse may leave you during the process.

At the end, God will turn this around.

I am led of the Lord not to talk cool nor conduct myself in a secular manner. I do not want to give into the format that "I'm taking back what the devil stole from me," by giving into worldly dancing, lust, or desiring prosperity rather than living Holy. Instead, I feel an urgency that Christians need to tune in to Jesus Christ. What are we doing for Christ? How are we blessing His kingdom? We need to pray more and tune into the Spirit of God.

Sometimes, people try to get to you by going after what they think will hurt you. Joseph's coat of many colors was stripped from him. After he was lowered into the pit, his brothers ate bread. They had no remorse. This it the difference between a man of God and unsaved men. Joseph was sold to the Egyptians. When Potiphar's wife tried to get him to sleep with her, Joseph fled and she tore a portion of his garment. She told the men of the house that he tried to force himself on her.

It was prophesied to me that I would be blessed. My wife and I were trying to locate a place to rent prior to relocating to Florida and it was difficult at first until the Lord gave us favor with a builder that also rented properties. My flesh did not like what I was going through. But God was with me (like He was with Joseph).

When you have the favor of God, you cannot expect man to be in favor of you unless God touches their heart. Your blessing is on the way. You have to be determined to win the race. I do not care what it looks or feels like, your blessing it on the way. Although it may appear as though it is not of God, it is. The enemy likes to mock God's people. What you are experiencing could be God preparing you for His purpose.

Someone prophesied that God is with me and I receive this.

CHAPTER THIRTEEN

Seek God's Wisdom. Be very astute in the word of God. My knowledge in the word of God should supercede my knowledge of computers. I say this due to my hobby of building computers in which I am knowledgeable. A person could have knowledge and not have wisdom. Wisdom will save you from men who are perverse.

Have mercy and truth. Do not tell lies and have compassion on others. Otherwise, the same judgment will come upon you. You will find favor in the sight of God and man.

Lk:2:52: And Jesus increased in wisdom and stature, and in favour with God and man.

Acts:2:47: Praising God, and having favour with all the people. And the Lord added to the church daily such as should be saved.

We like to snatch this scripture from this section and apply all of our problems. Wisdom is action. First, you have to be an open receptacle to receive wisdom, and then apply it.

If you remember the older generation's sayings, it is really the word of God, e.g., "Whatever goes around comes around." The word of God says:

Gal:6:7: Be not deceived; God is not mocked: for whatsoever a man soweth, that shall he also reap.

The enemy will attack your mind with scenarios, imagery, and the like to the point where it is as if you are watching a movie. The enemy attacked my mind this past week. I was driving a garbage truck and I looked out the passenger window and noticed a bent mailbox lying on the ground. The devil played tricks on my mind and tried to make it appear as though I was the cause.

I questioned my co-worker that was with me at the time as to whether I did this and he replied, "No." Later that evening, I wrestled with fear and torment. The enemy tried to convince me to lie and cheat with threats that my supervisor would be calling me regarding this. I began to meditate on God's word. I knew that I did not hit the mailbox. The devil tried to get me to commit sin. I began to trust God. My supervisor called me on the radio the following day and inquired as to how I was doing. Everything was fine. You have to apply the wisdom of God to your life. You are practicing wisdom when you apply the word of God in your life. Do not allow the chastening of God to pull you out of the wisdom of God. It does not matter whether you are humiliated; do not allow anything to pull you from the wisdom of God.

Some people become bombarded with situations and do nothing. Some people panic and scream while others take in the word of God and walk in His wisdom. I learned to chasten my daughter with wisdom. Wisdom will lead you to address a situation without making the other individual feel withdrawn. The wisdom of God will draw your family in. God's word will not return unto Him void.

Job:38:36: Who hath put wisdom in the inward parts? or who hath given understanding to the heart?

Someone was trying to tell me what is of God and what is not. You will only know that for yourself. When people question me as to whether something is of God in another person's life, I would not know without praying and receiving an answer from the Lord, or the individual does something according to the word of God or does something contrary to the word of God. I can discern whether there is an evil spirit involved. We do not need to worry about where another individual stands in the Lord. Only that individual and God knows.

Prov:3:23: 23: Then shalt thou walk in thy way safely, and thy foot shall not stumble.

The Bible promises us pleasantness, peace, length of days, riches and honor. Wisdom is more precious than jewels and nothing is comparable to it.

Wisdom will keep you from making the same mistakes twice and from making the mistakes that others have made.

Prov:3:13: Happy is the man that findeth wisdom, and the man that getteth understanding.

CHAPTER FOURTEEN

I will say, yes Lord—whatever you are
requiring of me. Joseph had a gift of dream
interpretation. Joseph interpreted the dream of
Pharaoh and that is when the blessings began to
flow. Gen:40:1-4, 25-47. God had Joseph in
Egypt for this cause:

Joseph's wife was there:

- To save the Egyptians from perishing;
- To save his family from perishing;
- To humble his brethren; and
- To be glorified in the lives of the Egyptians
  and Joseph's family.

The Spirit of the Lord spoke to me this
morning and showed me His saints seeking Him
for material blessings. We are experiencing a
change. The Lord changed me when he
relocated me to prepare for His work.

I told the Lord that I am always doing
something for others and never having time for

myself. The Lord showed me that He is preparing me to be kingdom minded.

While driving my work truck, a man told me to slow down, and my flesh rose. I said within my heart, "Yes Lord," then I replied to the man, "Yes," then I slowed down.

We have to put off our flesh. We need to seek God about the processes we are experiencing. I am not seeking a two million membership because I want to be able to minister to the church members effectively.

Jesus gave purpose to Simon (Peter) and Andrew his brother when He told them to follow Him. When you find yourself griping about a situation, do something about it. We have to be girded with truth. Show me in the word of God where the enemy is supposed to snatch your joy, etc. The enemy is supposed to be under your feet. The enemy is constantly trying to get out from under your feet. We have small reptiles in Florida that are very agile. That is the way the enemy is. You have to keep him under your feet.

Salvation is not for the fearful. It is for the brave at heart. You have to want this! That is similar to seeing a muscular man being intimidated and being a wimp. You have the power and authority. Do not sulk because you have to go through something. Do not allow the enemy to trick you into believing you are not Holy Ghost filled. If you spoke in other tongues when you received the Holy Ghost, then you were filled.

Begin cutting off things that do not edify. Whenever I pray, I pray audibly. I realize that that I do not have to pray audibly. However, I feel the devil back off me whenever I pray loud and forcibly in doing spiritual warfare.

This walk is not for show. It is for eternal life. Everyone will spend eternity somewhere. Where do you want to end up? You have to give up the world including worldly music. What type of soldier is that going to make you?

When you find yourself in a situation where you want to backbite; remember there is never a time for backbiting. Pray for the brethren and others. You have to step out in faith and decide you are not going to allow your circumstances dictate to you.

God has called me to be a warrior! Joseph did not break when he was in prison. God will give you peace in the midst of all your troubles.

Stop trying to figure it out and allow God to take you through. If you stand your ground, God will show you His salvation (your deliverance). Just stand your ground and God will deliver and set free. You cannot be fearful!

You may think, I'm not going to let them talk to me that way. Take heed, let the word of God change you and people will change. Let Him change your attitude by saying, yes Lord, to your will and submitting to His will. Joseph yielded to God's will. Remember, Potiphar's wife lied on him. Count it all joy, know that God is with you, and will carry you through.

I was driving the garbage truck and working with some immigrant non-English speaking men. They are fully aware that I stand for Jesus Christ although they do not speak English. I was blessed with a forty-dollar tip and one of the workers replied, "Good Jesus," which he pronounced the name Jesus to sound like *"HeySeuss,"* (phonetically spelled). The Lord is using me to be a witness to the men. They are beginning to inquire about visiting the church.

We may need to have the sermons translated for them to receive Jesus Christ as their Lord and savior. I am having this book translated in Spanish for this reason.

CHAPTER FIFTEEN

I shall praise the Lord at all times. We are a chosen generation that should show forth the praises of Him who have called us from darkness.

Saints, abstain from lusts that war against the soul, casting down imaginations. There is nothing good about the imagination I mentioned this earlier. We imagine ourselves to be exalted rather than being humbled.

Living in a fantasy world is not of God. It never allows ourselves to be humble. We are to walk in humility and walk upright before God. It is not like the days of old, when the Holy Spirit had not yet been given prior to the Upper Room. We have the Holy Spirit dwelling within us and therefore are required to live Holy. There is no excuse not to live Holy. The Lord expects nothing less than holiness without which we will not see the Lord – at least not in peace!

Rom:6:22: But now being made free from sin, and become servants to God, ye have your fruit unto holiness, and the end everlasting life.

2Cor:7:1: Having therefore these promises, dearly beloved, let us cleanse ourselves from all filthiness of the flesh and spirit, perfecting holiness in the fear of God.

The Bible tells us to submit ourselves to every ordinance of man for the Lord's sake.

1Pt:2:13: Submit yourselves to every ordinance of man for the Lord's sake: whether it be to the king, as supreme;

After finishing my route early one Saturday morning around 11:00 a.m., and realizing that I did not have to give my son a ride prior to heading home, my supervisor radioed me and asked me to assist another worker. My supervisor informed me that he was sending a better truck with another helper. I became quiet and thought within my heart, I want to show forth the praises of God at all times with my life who has called me out of darkness. I replied, "Okay," and agreed to work late. A moment later, my supervisor called me again, and thanked me then said I could leave early. What if I would have displayed a nasty attitude? God would not have been glorified. This is only for a season. I realize that I am not going to always do this for a living.

Nevertheless, while I am performing this task, I will glorify God. Even if I had to work over, God would have blessed me in that situation.

There would be no advancement if it were not for Jesus being our foundation. Remember our enemy is clever. The enemy will bring up our past in an attempt to condemn.

Should you slip, repent and trust in Jesus Christ. When the enemy thinks he has you, the Lord will make a way of escape. Pick up your sword, shield, and helmet and go on. It is impossible to do this without the Holy Ghost. Do not allow anything to cause you to lay your weapons down. Do not do it!

We praise God by being complete examples of holiness to show the praises of God. Christ did not threaten people! Some saints believe that it okay to threaten people.

1Pt:2:17: Honour all men. Love the brotherhood. Fear God. Honour the king.

Through the beauty of Christ, He changed my desires and my wicked ways. My wife always hated when I used to flirt after other women. God changed me. It will pay off if you give up your flesh for the prize of Christ!

You need to go through every extent to win that soul for Christ. You have to be that example. You have to win souls for Christ in your home first by being the right example and speaking the word of God.

You have to be willing to get dirty for the Lord by being a servant. You cannot always look to your schedule. You have to be a soldier. You have to view situations the way Jesus did. What is wrong with your capabilities? Do not be a wimp and quit. When you think that people are always picking on you and talking about you, you decide to quit or give up. When you quit, you get nothing! You have to be a servant of God, willing to serve. Get out of your flesh and serve God. Put your will out of your mind, but give your will to Jesus. Humble yourself to serve.

My first job was a dishwasher. I made certain the dishes were clean and ready to be used in the restaurant. I serve with humility gathering garbage throughout neighborhoods in various weather conditions. I have gathered dirty laundry for people even when it was unfair. Stop telling Jesus that He has to do it another way – be a servant. If you have to miss dinner to pray for someone, do it. God will prepare a table for you in the presence of your enemies. Serve God's people. Everyone is God's people – saved and unsaved. When people inquire, "Why do you do this so humbly?" Use this as an opener to witness about Jesus Christ.

We have no excuse for not being saved. When Jesus died on the cross, He gave us power. We have also been given a measure of faith. You do not have to develop your faith progressively or in a process unless you choose to. If you have faith as a grain of mustard seed, you do not have to go through a process. You just have to step up to the plate and hit a home run of faith and stop allowing the ball to whiz pass. If you believe God for a job, when He blesses you with it, work it! Even if you feel it is not your job, be faithful. Moreover, if it is not your job, Jesus will move you to another job. Jesus did all that He was going to do on the cross when He gave us the victory. Jesus conquered this world through His death on the cross and gave you the same victory! If you have a problem or need, Jesus gave you power and faith to believe Him to supply your need. He gave you the power to speak nice things when people speak evil unto you. God gave you power and authority. You are successful when you walk upright before the Lord and walk in faith.

Saints are always looking to be delivered. Christ died unto sin once – meaning that everything you need was provided when He was nailed to the cross. Rom:6:10. He provided your salvation, deliverance, healing, etc. He is not going to climb up on the cross again. He died unto sin once. You do not have to wait to be delivered! Christ made you free. Walk therein.

Be not entangled again in the yoke on bondage! Therefore, do not yield your members (body parts) to sin. If you do, you become a servant or a slave to sin. Walk in newness of life. The old man is dead to sin! We have been given a new nature; we are new creatures in Christ.

The wages of sin is death. Rom:6:23. Do not let sin rule you. It does not matter what your background is, including the type of family you came from. Christ nailed this to the cross including your shame. There is no more condemnation! You are free! Live victoriously!

We are a power-packed dynamo with the Armour of God on. Jesus told us to take up our cross and follow Him. This is how you take up your cross:

Firstly, you must deny yourself and follow Jesus. Secondly, conquer the impulses to sin (subdue, conquer, pull down, vanquish).

Mt:16:24: Then said Jesus unto his disciples, If any man will come after me, let him deny himself, and take up his cross, and follow me.

- Protect your mind with the Helmet of Salvation

- Have the Sword of the Spirit which is the word of God

- Put on the Breastplate of Righteousness

- Possess the Shield of Faith

- Girt your loins with Truth

- Feet shod with the preparation of the Gospel of Peace (be prepared to proclaim the Gospel)

Eph.6:11: Put on the whole armour of God, that ye may be able to stand against the wiles of the devil.

Eph.6:12: For we wrestle not against flesh and blood, but against principalities, against powers, against the rulers of the darkness of this world, against spiritual wickedness in high places.

Eph.6:13: Wherefore take unto you the whole armour of God, that ye may be able to withstand in the evil day, and having done all, to stand.

Eph.6:14: Stand therefore, having your loins girt about with truth, and having on the breastplate of righteousness;

Eph.6:15: And your feet shod with the preparation of the gospel of peace;

Eph.6:16: Above all, taking the shield of faith, wherewith ye shall be able to quench all the fiery darts of the wicked.

Eph.6:17: And take the helmet of salvation, and the sword of the Spirit, which is the word of God:

Eph.6:18: Praying always with all prayer and supplication in the Spirit, and watching thereunto with all perseverance and supplication for all saints;

CHAPTER SIXTEEN

This new-fangled preaching that we are hearing is not of God. I received my foundation from a church where the pastor taught from the word of God. I was taught to put off the flesh and to live holy. When I hear preachers tell their congregation that they do not have to preach living holy and dying to the flesh anymore, it sounds depressing and I am not depressed.

It is like having a computer to function without the motherboard. I hear people in public talk as though it is okay to commit sin and serve God.

I observed a saint with a stack of lottery tickets. I inquired, "What are you doing with those lotto tickets?"

He said, "I got to have some leisure time."

You need to have the word of God in your very being, in your life, and in your marrow.

We honor and prep this flesh. It is the flesh that is binding. Who wants to be bound when you can stay free? I will reiterate the fact that Christ made you free. Do not become entangled again with the yoke of bondage!

Gal:5:1: Stand fast therefore in the liberty wherewith Christ hath made us free, and be not entangled again with the yoke of bondage.

There are preachers teaching saints to look to themselves and prosperity messages. Firstly, there is no good thing in this flesh. Secondly, the flesh will fail you. Some saints cannot fast for a week or even a day. The flesh has the victory when you give in to it.

Again, saints cannot talk to people any way they feel and still be saved. Jesus changed the law that rendered an eye for an eye and a tooth for a tooth. He voided this law. We are to be Christ-like.

Anytime we do something, we expect grace but do not want to render grace. God says to love your brethren, not just the people you want to love or only the members of your church. We cannot pick and choose who we extend the Gospel to.

We need to be committed to the faith. I stopped preaching using the Greek and Hebrew meanings. We need to preach the word of God as it is written. When you know someone is wrong and you take their side, you are wrong too. The people that are receiving salvation today want to be saved. God is transferring people throughout this nation. Some may think they are displaced due to the impact from hurricanes and other adverse conditions. We need to ensure that the people have a place to worship God.

I was feeling weary in my body and my flesh told me to take it easy and not to preach so hard today. I preached hard anyway with just a few people in the ministry because my flesh does not have the victory!

God is not playing in these last days! The devil is playing for keeps. Saints that are not living holy will be left behind when the Lord gets ready to make a spiritual move to prepare for His return. I am not speaking of the catching away of the saints. I am speaking of when the Lord moves upon those that He has called to do an end-time work.

Do not allow the world to define who you are in Jesus Christ. Jesus loves you. Stop allowing situations and environments to define who you are. If you trust and allow Jesus, He will define who you are.

For example, I work as a garbage man (although I am a senior pastor). Being a garbage man does not define who I am. God defines me as being His servant and His prophet. I am a holy man of God.

Sometimes, people will try to place their definitions on you. They may make comments like, e.g., "I don't like that outfit on you." If you like the outfit, wear it. I am not speaking of something that displays your uncomely parts. However, I think you get the picture.

If you are working in a hostile environment, do not become hostile, continue to treat people with love. You cannot go into a place to minister to prostitutes, drug dealers, etc., if you have a hidden desire to participate in these things.

You expect the world to love you; you are not of this world. You cannot expect the world to understand and love you. You cannot accept the advice from the ungodly.

Do not concern yourself with what the world has to say about you.

Ps:1:1: Blessed is the man that walketh not in the counsel of the ungodly, nor standeth in the way of sinners, nor sitteth in the seat of the scornful.

When you choose not to follow the world, they crucify you. When you choose not to do right in the eyes of the Lord, you can repent! This is why I am uncomfortable accepting monies from the government concerning faith-based initiatives. The Lord may have me to move in a certain way and the government may not agree to it. That is precisely why I do not want their funding.

Churches, mega-churches, homes, etc., were being constructed prior to the faith-based monies being available because Jesus was blessing in these areas—not the government!

Allow Jesus to define who you are. Allow Him to dry your tears of disappointment.

Praising God should not be difficult. It helps dry those tears.

Speaking in tongues should not be a task either. Many saints cannot praise God unless the pastor is present. This should not be. We are not serving a ministry, nor the pastor(s), we are serving God. Without the Lord, I am nothing. If you are the only one giving God praise, do not worry about the congregation. Just lead praise service or give God your praise in the sanctuary or wherever you are!

Do not worry about the crowd or how you sound; just rely on the Lord. If someone asks, what do you have to praise God for? Everyone should have something to praise God for. What is the difference if the praise leader asks, What has the Lord done for you?

You should be able to give the Lord praise and have a testimony. I believe that there are saints that feel when they come to church they do not have to share their testimony. You are denying your brethren the opportunity to grasp hold to faith. Your testimony strengthens the brethren.

Lk:22:32: But I have prayed for thee, that thy faith fail not: and when thou art converted, strengthen thy brethren.

When you are hurting, you as well as the other saints can praise Jesus in the midst of your trouble and the blessing is sweet. Saints can also pray for you. There is no excuse for not sharing your testimony. Even if you are running for your life, there is still praise in knowing the Lord can keep you. You can give God the praise through anything.

What do you come to church for if you do not want to give God praise? It should be easy to praise God. Even if you have to go into your archives, you should have praises for God. If you do not have anything to praise God for in your archives, there is something wrong with your Christian walk. Each day you live, God is doing something in your life. Realize what you are here for and what God has called you to do. It should not be hard for you to voice that. You should not have to contemplate about the goodness of the Lord. The Lord has brought me off the streets, off crack-cocaine, from prison, etc., to give Him glory. Last night I was sick with a terrible cough and the Lord delivered me. Does that deserve praise? Yes it does. The Lord is always worthy of my praise. He is my life.

CHAPTER SEVENTEEN

Without faith, it is impossible to please God.

Heb:11:6: But without faith it is impossible to please him: for he that cometh to God must believe that he is, and that he is a rewarder of them that diligently seek him.

Everyone places their trust in what they have obtained. Job gives a good example of what could occur at any point in your life. Someone can come to you with bad news.

Your employers can tell you that your job is being transferred to Mexico. Where do you place your trust? The Lord has placed in my heart that you can lose these things at anytime.

You should never lose your faith nor your trust in God. Job got on his knees, shaved his head and still gave God praise. God will always be there for you. You have to remember that whenever things go wrong or you receive bad news, God will be there for you.

Do not place your faith in the things you have obtained. Put your faith in the one that provided you the job.

Peter walked on water until he was distracted. You cannot allow the things in this life to distract you from what God has bidded you to do.

When the crowd is not at your ministry, you have to keep your eyes on Jesus by faith. I started this church with just my four family members. The crowd is not here under the ministry at this time. My faith is in God. You must believe and exercise your faith! Where do you place your faith this morning? Do you place faith in your husband and his job and your children that you imparted everything to?

Your goal should be as Job said, *"For all I know that my Redeemer liveth and that He shall stand at the latter day upon the earth: and though after my skin worms destroy this body, yet in my flesh shall I see God." Job:19:25-26.*

We should seek to bless others as God has blessed us. Remember where your abundance comes from. God is getting ready to open some magnificent doors. We need to understand that it is God. When Job's wife tried to get him to curse God, Job explained to her that if she could accept the good from God, she could also accept the bad. The job you possess right now means nothing unless God is touching it. The same goes for your house you live in, your clothing, and the food you consume. You must reverence God.

This is not a group thing. God will judge individuals – not groups. Albeit things do happen in strong numbers and you are able to conquer in strong numbers. Another part of our assignment is to get the saints back that have been captured by the enemy and to bring in people that have not received salvation.

What do you place your trust in? We all have hobbies and things we enjoy doing. None of these things compare to the things of God.

We were poor when I was a child. Our windows had air pockets and we could hear the air make whistling noises that sounded creepy. Do not allow yourself to be shaken. Place your trust in Jesus Christ. Remember where your blessings come from. It is by faith that you please Him. Remember who to place your trust in — Jesus Christ. He paid the ultimate price for your soul.

When the Lord starts to bless you, remember who it is that blessed you. Do not make your job, house, children, etc., idols. Some people fear losing their job. You cannot afford to lose your soul. You can afford to lose everything else! What do you place your trust in?

CHAPTER EIGHTEEN

Why do you need salvation? Some saints believe they need Jesus Christ to "Just get me through another day Lord." Your state of mind should be that you want your soul to spend an eternity with Jesus.

You cannot save yourself. How long will God suffer with you? I admonish you to seek the Lord while He may be found.

There was a time when people of God separated themselves from others that did not live holy, and from those the Lord turned into reprobate minds. I asked myself this morning, how long will God suffer with me in my disobedience? We need to be saved. You want to be saved so that your soul will enter into the New Jerusalem. You want to live holy so that people can see your witness. You need to be saved so that you can move on with your life in Christ – not this trick life. You need salvation so that you may function as God's creation.

You have the authority to call things that are not as though they were by faith through Jesus Christ.

Rom:4:17: (As it is written, I have made thee a father of many nations,) before him whom he believed, even God, who quickeneth the dead, and calleth those things which be not as though they were.

You need the precious Holy Ghost so that you can wash your mind and be filled with the things of God. Some think that you automatically change. There are still some things that enter your mind. You have to cast those things down that try to plague your mind. You have to cast down all evil thoughts.

The world is wicked and many of the people in it are wicked. Individuals that do not implement the word of God nor the things that be of God are in charge of the monetary systems including the work places. Older movies used to have characters that would call on Jesus or God in certain scenes or perhaps quote a scripture. People who chose a gay lifestyle are designing clothing. You have to be led of the Lord as what to wear. That is why you see some outfits that you do not want to wear because they are ungodly.

All flesh has sinned and come short of the glory of God. Jesus can save your soul and deliver you. It is time out for preachers trying to use creative ways to present the word of God. They need to preach and teach the word of God as it is written. There is no one or nothing that can touch you like Jesus. He can make you feel good like no one can.

There is no other faith or religion that can do you like Jesus. Jesus Christ is the only way. All have sinned and need to be saved. It does not matter what race you are. Jesus loves you and is calling for you to be saved.

We need to let people know they need to be saved. People need to know that Jesus is real!

CHAPTER NINETEEN

I want to talk about Christian Testing. If you are going through something, go through for the sake of Christ. Yes, my mother passed away. Nevertheless, I learned that Jesus is all things to me. When you no longer have someone like your mother to stroke you when you do well, apply the word of God. I did.

You no longer have any excuse for having a bad attitude when you go through testing. You cannot fail at allowing people to see you as a minister or a servant of Christ at all times. At no time should you exalt the devil. At no time should profanity proceed from you. You have to be constantly aware of what or whom you are exalting. Is what you are saying or doing exalting the name of Jesus? If you are saved, you are a minister of the word. We have to be careful and exalt the word of God and the things of God.

The disciples disconnected themselves from the things of this world. We want to exalt the movie we watched, the game you watched last night, your favorite idol, movie stars, etc.

You will have power if you disconnect yourself from the cares of this world. When saints question me as to why they do not possess the power and yet others do. I explain it is because you have not allowed the Lord to separate you, roll you up, and then release you similar to the metamorphic process a caterpillar experiences prior to becoming a butterfly.

We do not want the Potter to shape and mold us. We do not want it like Apostle Paul and Peter received the power. We want everything microwave fast. I have heard people compare themselves with Paul. Paul was beaten with rods, shipwrecked, in perils of robbers, in perils of his own fellow citizens, perils by heathens, in perils in the city, in perils in the wilderness, the sea and among false brethren, in weariness, coldness, nakedness and hunger!

2Cor:11:26: In journeyings often, in perils of waters, in perils of robbers, in perils by mine own countrymen, in perils by the heathen, in perils in the city, in perils in the wilderness, in perils in the sea, in perils among false brethren;

2Cor:11:27: In weariness and painfulness, in watchings often, in hunger and thirst, in fastings often, in cold and nakedness.

Paul explained that if he must glory, he will glory in his infirmities. Preachers need to come out from behind the pulpits and out of their comfort zones and get out in the streets in the city and reach the lost.

Most saints have church faith. We need to have international faith. We need to minister to the people on the outside, i.e., people that do not have any direction. God is calling for people to serve Him whole heartily.

We know that the heart is the mind. When you choose to serve God with all your might – all hell will break lose! You have to make up your mind whether you truly want to be saved. We need to accept the word of God as the word of God. We need not to be ashamed of the Gospel of Jesus Christ! Jesus said if you are ashamed of Him, He will be ashamed of you.

Mk:8:38: Whosoever therefore shall be ashamed of me and of my words in this adulterous and sinful generation; of him also shall the Son of man be ashamed, when he cometh in the glory of his Father with the holy angels.

Are you aware that you can sit in church and be in sin perhaps as a gambler, lustful, etc.?

If you get in the realm of God and give up everything that you value as being pleasurable, you will lose your friends. What in this life is worth having so important to lose your soul for? Is it to build an empire, a new hotel, etc.? All of these things will perish and you will not have another chance once God passes judgment.

Nothing should stop you from serving God. I recall a preacher that used to preach about not allowing anything to prevent you from attending church services including the death of a loved one. There is something wrong when I read about Paul's suffering and I see preachers being worshipped and exalted.

Remember to love and serve Christ with all your heart and mind.

CHAPTER TWENTY

Loving Christ is power! Through loving Christ, you have power to heal the sick. Not only does it take faith; it takes love to desire to help anyone. How can you love Christ if you do not love one another? In loving Christ, you do not have to go lacking. In just loving Him, you do not have to concern yourself with the cares of this life. In loving Christ, it causes selfishness to flee. In loving Christ, you do not have to concern yourself with nuclear bombs or explosions because you know He will make everything all right. In loving Christ, you know that you have a place in Him.

Before you can actually have power in Christ, you must first love Him. We always hear people talk about that fact that Jesus loves us. What about loving Him? I have compiled several scriptures pertaining to this, in which I chose not to list them all.

The reason many do not possess power in Jesus is because He has to be first. Most people are like this, I love my neighbor, but I don't necessarily have to associate with him.

Nevertheless, if he needs me, I will help him. If I love my neighbor as I love myself (I think about myself often), I will think about my neighbor often. We have been messed up when it comes to loving God.

I read the news where a little girl was walking down the street and noticed the neighbor's door open. The little girl told her mother about the door and they went to check on the neighbor. They found the neighbor passed out with a circular saw in his leg. He was a paramedic, but could not help himself. How many people would have done this? Most people would have thought this was none of their business and would not have checked to learn why their neighbor's door was open.

Ps:37:4: Delight thyself also in the LORD; and he shall give thee the desires of thine heart.

Jesus should be our first thought in the morning and when calamity comes and tries to overshadow the anointing. Because we love Him, He can preserve us by just loving Him. In loving God, there is power for you to change because in loving God, you desire to change and not allow anything to stop you. When you have trouble in your marriage, God will alleviate the pressure. I have been in situations and was not clever enough to deliver myself. Nevertheless, God was able to deliver me. When I begin to think, I love you Jesus, when I am engulfed in situations, He stops whatever is trying to defeat me! I love to think on how much I love Jesus.

In loving Jesus, you do not have to think about how the way is going to be made. He gives you victory through loving Him. You do not have to worry about your child not acting right. You do not have to worry about the cares of this life. God gave His only begotten Son.

We do not have to accept the things that the devil is trying to put on us, e.g., trying to make you gay, wanting you to carry a pistol, etc. Jesus is your "pistol." Apply the word of God. Rather than complain about not having power, try loving God and see how much power you possess. Loving God gives you power. Just touch the hem of His garment in the spirit. Cast all your cares upon Him. I have nothing to worry about. God has kept me and He shall keep you.

When you go into your supervisor's office and he hands you a layoff notice, the enemy starts to creep in and tells you about your bills that are due. That is when your inner man should kick in and tell you because you love God, He will make a way. The layoff notice can be a promotion for the job Jesus has that you truly desire. We need to stand on our faith and love God. Sometimes this fleshly body does not want to respond correctly. The body can become comatose. You have to love God in your heart. When I think about the City of the New Jerusalem, I just love Jesus. It may sound a little crazy, but I just love Him. That is where my power comes in through love.

I recall when the enemy brought it to my attention that a problem was there, the Lord had already solved it. If you truly love God, you would know that. There is power and victory in loving God. There is also perseverance. Keep it going and do not look back—no matter if you feel you cannot take it. Do not look back. Love God with all your heart. There was a woman in the scriptures that looked back (Lot's wife) and turned into a pillar of salt. Remember, there is no repentance in the grave!

Gen:19:26: But his wife looked back from behind him, and she became a pillar of salt.

Lord, let thy will be done. Jonah was a prophet of God. We as preachers sometimes think that we are higher than saints and sinners. Sometimes pastors have a tendency to pass judgment. Sometimes preachers and prophets have a tendency to tell God when they think that people are undeserving of His blessings.

I will not prevent anyone from doing what God has instructed them to do or become. If anyone tells me they feel the call of God on their life, I will not stand in their way.

Everyone has been through something in their lives – some worse than others. Jonah was a man of God and knew the power of God. He was irate because God wanted to have mercy upon the people of Nineveh, that great city where there were more than 120,000 people.

You must have mercy when you call yourself being a man or woman of God. Jonah found himself in a precarious situation and desired the Lord to deliver him. He cried out to the Lord and humbled himself. Jonah was disobedient and did not want God to deliver the Ninevites.

However, when God allowed Jonah to be swallowed in the belly of the great fish, he wanted God to save him and be merciful. Afterwards, Jonah heard from the Lord again requesting him to do his bidding. Jonah obeyed and prophesied to the people of Nineveh. The king and all the people of Nineveh fasted and repented of their evil deeds. Therefore, God was merciful and decided not to destroy them. Jonah still felt that the people were undeserving of God's mercy. Afterwards, Jonah was grieved and wanted to die. The Lord prepared a gourd to provide shade and comfort for Jonah. The following morning, the Lord prepared a worm to destroy the gourd. Jonah became upset again, this time about the gourd being destroyed. God questioned Jonah regarding his anger over the gourd that was destroyed and concerning the fact that Jonah should have the same pity on the people of Nineveh that he had for the gourd.

God wants everyone to be saved. He is not willing that anyone should perish. Who are we to judge and decide whom God is to show mercy? That is why God is God. He desires every man to inherit eternal life with Him. We have to take a stand as people of God to do what He has called us to do. It is time out for being selfish.

1Cor:10:24: Let no man seek his own, but every man another's wealth.

It is time out for being selfish and self-centered. Who fulfills the scripture quoted above? My desire is for souls to be saved, and that saints will fast, pray, seek God, and stop lusting for material things as being most important. We have to draw people with love and kindness. All people matter and they need to know that Jesus is real!

I pray that this book has given you biblical insight to develop a true spiritual mind for life that you may live victoriously in Jesus Christ – being perfect and lacking nothing.

—Dr. J. Maximillian Thurmond